Learn Microsoft® Excel® 2010 and 2013 for Windows® in 2

Copyright © Liaw Hock Sang 2015

Trademarks and Copyrighted Content

Every effort has been made to appropriately capitalize all terms that are known to be trademarks or service marks mentioned in this book. The author cannot attest to the accuracy of this information. Use of a term in this book should not be regarded as affecting the validity of any trademark or service mark. All screenshots used are at the best effort not to violate the copyrighted content of Microsoft® or any parties. Should there be any violations in this respect, the author apologies and shall stop the selling of the book **Learn Microsoft® Excel® 2010 and 2013 for Windows® in 24 Hours** within the control of the author.

Microsoft, Excel, Word, Visual Basic, and Windows are either registered trademarks or trademarks of Microsoft Corporation in the United States and/or other countries. All other trademarks and trade names are the property of their respective owners.

Warning and Disclaimer

Every effort has been made to make this book as accurate as possible. However, no warranty or fitness is implied. The author and the publisher shall have neither responsibility nor liability to any person or entity with respect to any losses or damages arising from the information contained in this book.

An Excel® File to Share

Thank you for purchasing this book. The author would like to share the Excel® file used in preparing the book. It includes all the working examples in the book – number formats, named formulas, formulas, ranges with conditional formatting, live calendars, a custom list of Roman numerals, data validation lists, controls on a worksheet, VBA code, and others. It definitely facilitates you to master the content of the book. Please email to: liawhocksang@gmail.com

Table of Contents

Introduction

Microsoft® Excel® has many features. To learn most of the features it will take you months, if not weeks. In this short book, I will introduce you some commonly used and interesting features that you may need to dig into more advanced books before knowing how to apply them.

This book is for Windows®-based users. All the steps, formulas, and VBA code in the book are written and carefully tested in Microsoft® Excel® 2010 and 2013 for Windows®.

I assumed that you are either a beginner or an average Excel® user. Nevertheless, I assumed that a beginner should know how to open and save an Excel® file, and know what a cell, a range of cells, a worksheet, a dialog box, and a control (button, check box ...) are.

I hope this book will serve as a quick reference to implement some interesting features. Let Excel® work for you and make your work more impressive and elegant.

An Excel® File to Share

The author would like to share the Excel® file used in preparing the book. It includes all the working examples in the book – number formats, named formulas, formulas, ranges with conditional formatting, live calendars, a custom list of Roman numerals, data validation lists, controls on a worksheet, VBA code, and others. It definitely facilitates you to master the content of the book. Please email to: liawhocksang@gmail.com

Chapter 1: Formatting

How to Display Large Numbers in Thousands and Millions

When dealing with large numbers, scaling them to thousands or millions will greater improve their readability. The numbers are only scaled on display. Calculations involving those cells containing the numbers are still using the actual unscaled numbers. Figure 1-1 shows some examples of scaled numbers by using custom number formats.

Actual number	On display	Custom format
66950800	66,950.80	#,##0.00,
66950800	66,950.80 k	#,##0.00," k"
66950800	66.95	#,##0.00,,
66950800	66.95 M	#,##0.00,," M"

Figure 1-1: Displaying numbers in thousands and millions.

To scale numbers to their thousands, execute the following steps:

1. Select the cells that you want the numbers to be scaled.

2. Press Ctrl+1 to display the Format Cells dialog box. Select the Number tab.

3. Select Custom in the Category list box and type the following number format code into the Type field to scale the numbers to their thousands:

```
#,##0.00,
```

The hash (#) character is a digit placeholder. It displays only significant digits, and does not display insignificant zeros. For example, a format code #.0 displays 0.5 as .5 since the zero in 0.5 is considered insignificant.

4. Click OK to close the Format Cells dialog box.

To scale numbers to their millions, use the following number format code:

```
#,##0.00,,
```

To scale numbers to their hundreds, use the following number format code:

```
#,##0"."00
```

A number format string in fact can have up to four sections of format codes, separated by semicolons. It enables you to define the format codes for positive numbers, negative numbers, zero values, and text in their respective sections, as shown below:

```
<Positive number>;<Negative number>;<Zero value>;<Text>
```

One way to learn custom number formats is to study the existing built-in number formats. Enter a number into any cell in a worksheet, press Ctrl+1 to display the Format Cells dialog box, select the Number tab, choose one of the format categories in the Category list box, and lastly select the Custom category to study the number format string in the Type field.

To learn more on custom number formats, you may try to access a web page provided by Microsoft® entitled *Create or delete a custom number format*. It provides guidelines with examples of codes on how to customize number formats for numbers, text strings, dates, and times.

How to Align a Currency Symbol in a Cell

A currency symbol can be properly aligned to the left of a cell by using the following custom number format codes:

```
$* #,##0.00;$* -#,##0.00
```

The asterisk (*) in the codes above means to repeat the next character, which is a space, to fill the column width. Figure 1-2 shows some examples of applying the custom number format codes to align the currency symbols to the left.

Actual number	On display	Custom format
0	$ 0.00	$* #,##0.00;$* -#,##0.00
1.5	$ 1.50	$* #,##0.00;$* -#,##0.00
1,224	$ 1,224.00	$* #,##0.00;$* -#,##0.00
-1,224	$ -1,224.00	$* #,##0.00;$* -#,##0.00

Figure 1-2: Currency symbols are aligned to the left.

To display negative numbers in parentheses, you may use the following number format codes:

```
_($* #,##0.00_);_($* (#,##0.00)
```

The underscore (_) in the codes above means to leave a space equal to the width of the next character, which is either an opening bracket or a closing bracket in this case. With these codes, positive and negative numbers are properly aligned (see Figure 1-3).

Actual number	On display	Custom format
0	$ 0.00	_($* #,##0.00_);_($* (#,##0.00)
1.5	$ 1.50	_($* #,##0.00_);_($* (#,##0.00)
1,224	$ 1,224.00	_($* #,##0.00_);_($* (#,##0.00)
-1,224	$ (1,224.00)	_($* #,##0.00_);_($* (#,##0.00)

Figure 1-3: Currency symbols are aligned to the left with negative numbers in parentheses.

4

In fact the codes above are part of the Accounting number format. To learn more, enter a number into any cell, press Ctrl+1, select the Accounting category on the Number tab, and then select the Custom category to study the codes in the Type field.

How to Create Numbered and Bulleted Lists

Numbered and bulleted lists in Microsoft® Word® can be emulated in Excel® by using custom number formats. Figure 1-4 shows an example.

```
1.   Vegetable
          o Asparagus
          o Broccoli
          o Carrot
          o Cauliflower
          o Ginger
          o Pumpkin
2.   Fruit
          o Apple
          o Apricot
3.   Diary
          o Butter
          o Cheese
          o Yogurt
```

Figure 1-4: Creating numbered and bulleted lists in Excel®.

The numbered list in Figure 1-4 is with the following number format code:

```
#". "
```

In the code above, the text – a dot and a space in this case – inside the double quotation marks is meant to be displayed.

The bulleted list is with the following number format code:

```
o @
```

The character at (@) is a text placeholder. The code above means to place in front the text with two characters – a bullet character and a space in this case.

The bullet character o is generated by pressing Alt+9 using the numeric keypad. To generate a solid bullet character •, press Alt+7. If your keyboard does not have the numeric keypad, an alternative is to insert the symbol by choosing Insert | Symbols | Symbol.

The bulleted lists in Figure 1-4 are in fact left indented too. To indent the content of a cell, select the cell, press Ctrl+1, and set a number in the Indent field on the Alignment tab.

Chapter 2: Formulas

How to Refer to a Constant or Text Without Occupying Any Cell

When working with worksheets you may repeatedly require a constant in your formulas. Often the constant is entered into a cell and it is then referred in the formulas. Alternatively, you may define a name for the constant, which does not occupy any cell.

To define a name for a constant, execute the following steps:

1. Choose Formulas | Defined Names | Define Name to display the New Name dialog box.

2. Type a name into the Name field for the constant.

   A defined name is not case-sensitive. For example, `InterestRate` is the same as `interestrate`.

3. In the Scope field, choose Workbook if you want to use the named constant in all worksheets in the workbook or choose a particular worksheet if you want to use it only in that worksheet.

4. Optional. Type something for your own reference into the Comment field.

5. Type the value of the constant with an equal sign before the constant, for example `=0.65`, into the Refers to field.

6. Click OK to close the New Name dialog box.

If cell A1 contains `1000` and `InterestRate` is a defined name for a constant with a value of 0.65, entering `=A1*InterestRate` into a cell returns `650`.

Similarly, we can define a name for text. Repeat the above steps, but, for example, type `NZ` into the Name field and `="New Zealand"` into the Refers to field. Enter the following formula into a cell:

```
="Product of " &NZ
```

The formula above returns the text `Product of New Zealand`. The ampersand (&) used in the formula is to concatenate the text `Product of` and the named text NZ.

The value of a named constant (whether for a number or text) can easily be changed by accessing the Name Manager dialog box (Ctrl+F3). Select the defined name, click Edit, and change the value of the constant in the Refers to field. All formulas using the constant will be then automatically recalculated. That's why named constants are preferable than hard core values when they are used in formulas.

How to Avoid Error Displays in Formulas and Why

Error displays in formulas, which are known as error values, provide valuable information and knowing what they mean can help us to rectify the errors quickly. Table 2-1 shows the error values and the reasons why they occur.

Table 2-1: Error values in formulas

Error value	Reason why it occurs
#NULL!	A non-existent range. You might have used an intersection operator (a space) to find an intersection between two ranges that do not intersect.
#DIV/0!	Excel® does not allowed a number to be divided by zero.
#VALUE!	A value of wrong data type.
#REF!	An invalid cell reference. The referred cell is either deleted or beyond the valid range of a worksheet. An invalid use of a cell reference also returns this error. For example, you enter =A3(1,2) into a cell. It is an invalid use of the cell reference A3.
#NAME?	A name that Excel® does not recognize. When text is not inside double quotation marks, Excel® tries to interpret it as a function name, a cell reference, or a defined name. When it fails, #NAME? is returned. You might get this error if your user defined functions are not properly installed or you use Excel® built-in functions that are only available in a later version of Excel®.
#NUM!	An invalid number. A typical example is taking the square root of a negative number.
#N/A	A value that is not available. For example, a lookup function (VLOOKUP, HLOOKUP, LOOKUP, or MATCH) does not find a match. Pasting values beyond the dimension of an array also returns this error.
#######	A negative date or time. Or a cell is not wide enough to display the result of a formula or of a custom format.

However, sometimes errors are expected and displaying them is trivial and even confusing to users. For example, the formula to calculate body-mass-index (BMI) is weight (in kilograms) divided by the square of height (in meters). With no data has been entered yet, the error #DIV/0! is expected in calculating BMI. Hence, it is more sensible to hide the error.

Let cell E4 contains the weight and cell E5 contains the height. To sensibly hide the error, use the following formula:

```
=IFERROR(E4/(E5*E5),"")
```

How to Know When to Use Relative, Absolute, and Mixed References

It depends on how you want a cell reference in a formula to vary when the formula is copied to other cells or evaluated in other cells of a selected range as in the case of conditional formatting.

A relative cell reference (for example, A1) allows both column and row parts of the reference to vary. An absolute cell reference (for example, $A$1) fixes both column and row parts of the reference by using two dollar signs. A mixed cell reference (for example, $A1 or A$1) fixes either column or row part of the reference.

You can best understand this concept by working through an example. Figure 2-1 shows the scores of three students obtained in their two quizzes: one with a full mark of 20 and the other with a full mark of 15. The weighting for the quiz assessment is 10%.

The formula to calculate the resultant score (in 10%) for the first student in cell E3 is:

`=$C$7*(C3/C$1+D3/D$1)/2`

	B	C	D	E
1	Full marks	20	15	
2	Name	Quiz 1	Quiz 2	Quiz (10%)
3	Stud1	20	15	10.0
4	Stud2	20	0	5.0
5	Stud3	10	15	
6				
7	Weighting (%)	10		

Figure 2-1: Using relative, absolute, and mixed references in a cell.

The formula in cell E3 is to be copied to the cells below. This formula uses an absolute reference for the weighting ($C$7), relative references for the scores (C3 and D3), and mixed references for the respective full marks (C$1 and D$1). As the formula is copied to the cells below, you want to have the weighting fixed (hence an absolute reference), the scores to vary accordingly to different students (hence relative references), and the row referring to the full marks fixed (hence mixed references).

This is a usual way of logic and it is nothing wrong using this logic to accomplish the task above. Alternatively, you may use mixed references for the scores ($C3 and $D3) and absolute references for the respective full marks ($C$1 and $D$1) since columns do not vary as the formula is copied to the cells below.

Note: You can press F4 to switch between relative, absolute, and mixed references.

How to Use Relative and Mixed References in Defined Names

Most often we use an absolute reference when defining a name for a cell or a range of cells. Nevertheless, a defined name can use a relative cell reference. For example, I am going to define a name called `Cell_U2L3`, which relatively points to a cell that is two rows up and three columns to the left from the cell where it is used.

To define the name `Cell_U2L3`, execute the following steps:

1. Select cell D6.

2. Choose Formulas | Defined Names | Define Name to display the New Name dialog box.

3. Type `Cell_U2L3` into the Name field.

4. In the Scope field, choose Workbook.

5. Type `=Chap2!A4` into the Refers to field or simply click cell A4 in the worksheet named Chap2 and press F4 few times to make A4 a relative reference.

   Note that cell A4 is 2 rows up and 3 columns to the left from cell D6.

6. Click OK to close the New Name dialog box.

Enter the following formula into any cell, for example cell E4:

```
=Cell_U2L3
```

The formula returns the value in cell B2, which is two rows up and three columns to the left from cell E4.

To understand the concept of defined name, regardless whether it is a named constant, a named cell, or a named range, it is better to treat the defined name as a named formula. Look at the Refers to field in the Name Manager of any name that has been defined, it is a formula! A formula always starts with an equal sign.

A named formula can also use mixed cell references. For example, I am going to define a named formula called `Cell_ColC_D1`, which relatively points to a cell that is in column C and one row down from the cell where it is used.

To define the named formula `Cell_ColC_D1`, execute the following steps:

1. Select cell E1.

2. Choose Formulas | Defined Names | Define Name to display the New Name dialog box.

3. Type `Cell_ColC_D1` into the Name field.

4. In the Scope field, choose Workbook.

5. Type `=Chap2!$C2`, which is a mixed reference, into the Refers to field.

6. Click OK to close the New Name dialog box.

Enter the following formula into any cell, for example cell F2:

```
=Cell_ColC_D1
```

The formula returns the value in cell C3, which is in column C and one row down from cell F2.

If you want a named formula that not just refers to the cells in a particular worksheet, delete the worksheet's name in the Refers to field. For example, I am going to define a named formula called `HalfoftheLeft`, which returns half of the value in a cell that is on the left of the cell where it is used.

To define the named formula `HalfoftheLeft`, execute the following steps:

1. Select cell E3.

2. Choose Formulas | Defined Names | Define Name to display the New Name dialog box.

3. Type `HalfoftheLeft` into the Name field.

4. In the Scope field, choose Workbook.

5. Type =!D3/2, which does not refer to any particular worksheet, into the Refers to field.

6. Click OK to close the New Name dialog box.

Enter the following formula into any cell in any worksheet to test the named formula:

`=HalfoftheLeft`

In fact a named formula is like other formulas that appear in the Formula bar. It can have more than one cell reference. It can also include Excel® built-in functions, user-defined functions, and even other named formulas. For example, I am going to define a named formula called AvgTop3of5, which returns the average of the 3 largest numbers out of 5 numbers.

To define the named formula AvgTop3of5, execute the following steps:

1. Select cell G2.

2. Choose Formulas | Defined Names | Define Name to display the New Name dialog box.

3. Type AvgTop3of5 into the Name field.

4. In the Scope field, choose Workbook.

5. Type the following formula into the Refers to field:

`=Average(Large(!B2:!F2,{1,2,3}))`

The formula takes the values in the 5 cells to the left of the cell where it is used and returns the average of the largest 3 by using the AVERAGE and LARGE functions.

6. Click OK to close the New Name dialog box.

Enter the following formula into any cell in any worksheet to test the named formula:

`=AvgTop3of5`

How to Find Duplicates Which Are Not Case Sensitive

To find duplicates which are not case sensitive in a range is straight forward by executing the following steps:

1. Select the range that you want to find duplicates.

2. Choose Home | Styles | Conditional Formatting | Highlight Cells Rules | Duplicate Values to display the Duplicate Values dialog box.

3. Click OK to accept the default settings.

Figure 2-2 shows an example of highlighted duplicates.

Duplicate entries (not case sensitive)			
26	76	P	P
91	41	A	Q
58	61	O	m
16	73	I	K
54	37	k	b
78	67	L	T
25	33	Y	M
68	16	]	C
66	63	K	H
64	53	c	V

Figure 2-2: Duplicates are highlighted using conditional formatting.

Conditional formatting is a powerful tool to visually present the contents of a range of cells when the contents meet certain rules or conditions that you set. A quick way to appreciate this feature is to explore the commands on the Home | Styles | Conditional Formatting drop-down list. Select a range of cells, click one of the commands, and accept the default settings. The result is instant.

How to Find Duplicates Which Are Case Sensitive

Figure 2-3 shows an example of highlighting case-sensitive duplicates.

	G	H	I	J
26	Duplicate entries (case sensitive)			
27	26	76	P	P
28	91	41	A	Q
29	58	61	O	m
30	16	73	I	K
31	54	37	k	b
32	78	67	L	T
33	25	33	Y	M
34	68	16	]	C
35	66	63	K	H
36	64	53	c	V

Figure 2-3: Finding case-sensitive duplicates using conditional formatting.

To find case-sensitive duplicates, execute the following steps:

1. Select the range in which duplicates are to find, G27:J36 in this case.

2. Choose Home | Styles | Conditional Formatting | New Rule to display the New Formatting Rule dialog box.

3. Select the rule type labeled Use a formula to determine which cells to format and type the following formula into the formula box labeled Format values where this formula is true:

   ```
   =SUM(1*(EXACT(G27,$G$27:$J$36)))>1
   ```

   The explanation to the above formula is quite lengthy. Please refer to the discussion after Step 5.

4. Click Format and choose the format that you want to apply if the formula returns TRUE.

5. Click OK twice to complete the conditional formatting.

18

Blank cells are duplicates too. To exclude the blank cells as duplicates, replace the formula in the formula box with the following formula:

```
=AND(G27<>"", SUM(1*(EXACT(G27,$G$27:$J$36)))>1)
```

A Discussion on the Formula in Step 3:

```
=SUM(1*(EXACT(G27,$G$27:$J$36)))>1
```

The EXACT function returns TRUE if the two arguments in the function are exactly the same. To understand what actually happens in EXACT(G27,$G$27:$J$36), the concept of array formula is needed. Cell G27 is compared with every cell in $G$27:$J$36. Consequently, an array of TRUEs and FALSEs is returned.

This array is then multiplied by 1 to create an array of 1s and 0s before they are summed with the SUM function. If the returned sum is greater than 1, then cell G27 is formatted according to the format you have set.

The conditional formatting is not only applied to cell G27. The above process is repeated to find the returned sum of every cell in the range G27:J36 selected in Step 1. In the formula in Step 3, G27 is a relative reference. Hence, its column and row parts are allowed to vary during the evaluation of the formula for every cell in the selected range. For example, during the evaluation of the formula for cell H28, the formula has actually become `=SUM(1*(EXACT(H28,$G$27:$J$36)))>1`.

To understand further about the results of the conditional formatting, execute the following steps:

1. Enter the following array formula into cell K27 by pressing Ctrl+Shift+Enter (not just Enter):

   ```
   =SUM(1*(EXACT(G27,$G$27:$J$36)))
   ```

2. Choose Formulas | Formula Auditing | Evaluate Formula to display the Evaluate Formula dialog box.

3. Click Evaluate few times and see how the evaluation is done in the Evaluation box before reaching the corresponding returned sum in cell G27.

4. To display the corresponding returned sums of other cells in the range G27:J36, drag the fill handle at the lower-right corner of cell K27 to copy the array formula to the cells below and to the cells on the left. The range K27:N36 is now filled with array formulas, which are used to find the corresponding returned sums in the range G27:J36.

	G	H	I	J	K	L	M	N
26	Duplicate entries (case sensitive)							
27	26	76	P	P	1	1	2	2
28	91	41	A	Q	1	1	1	1
29	58	61	O	m	1	1	1	1
30	16	73	I	K	2	1	1	2
31	54	37	k	b	1	1	1	1
32	78	67	L	T	1	1	1	1
33	25	33	Y	M	1	1	1	1
34	68	16	]	C	1	2	1	1
35	66	63	K	H	1	1	2	1
36	64	53	c	V	1	1	1	1

Figure 2-4: Checking results of conditional formatting with array formulas.

How to Determine the Date of a Particular Day in a Month

For example, what is the date of the second Wednesday in May? With the year in cell A1, enter the following formula into a cell:

```
=DATE(A1,5,1)+IF(4>=WEEKDAY(DATE(A1,5,1)),4-
 WEEKDAY(DATE(A1,5,1)),7-(WEEKDAY(DATE(A1,5,1))-
 4))+7*(2-1)
```

The formula consists of three parts. The first is the date for the first day of May. The second is an if-then-else statement. It determines the number of days needed to be added to the first day of May. The last is to add a multiple of 7.

To find the date of other day in a month, you may appropriately change the day, the month, and the year in the formula above. For example, to determine the third Thursday in June, replace the 5 with 6 (for June), the 4 with 5 (for Thursday), and the 2 with 3 (for the third week).

How is then the second last Wednesday in May determined? Here is the formula:

```
=DATE(A1,6,1)+IF(4>=WEEKDAY(DATE(A1,6,1)),4-
 WEEKDAY(DATE(A1,6,1)),7-(WEEKDAY(DATE(A1,6,1))-4))-
 7*2
```

The formula calculates the date for the first Wednesday in June, not May, and then 14 is subtracted from that date in order to reach the date in May.

How to Create a Live Calendar

A Monthly Live Calendar

Figure 2-5 shows an example of a monthly calendar created in a range of cells. It shows the calendar for May 2015 in the range B12:H19.

	B	C	D	E	F	G	H
12			May, 2015				
13	Sun	26	3	10	17	24	31
14	Mon	27	4	11	18	25	1
15	Tue	28	5	12	19	26	2
16	Wed	29	6	13	20	27	3
17	Thu	30	7	14	21	28	4
18	Fri		1	8	15	22	29	5
19	Sat	2	9	16	23	30	6

Figure 2-5: A live monthly calendar created in a range of cells.

To create the calendar, execute the following steps:

1. Select B12:H12 and merge the cells by choosing Home | Alignment | Merge & Center.

2. Enter the following formula into the merged cells:

   ```
   =DATE($B$1,5,1)
   ```

   Cell B1 contains the year (2015 in this example).

3. Select the merged cells and press Ctrl+1 to display the Format Cells dialog box. Select the Custom category on the Number tab and enter the following custom format into the Type field:

   ```
   mmmm, yyyy
   ```

   The code mmmm is to display the month name in full and the code yyyy is to display the year in four digits. To display an abbreviated month name, use mmm.

4. Enter the abbreviated day names in the range B13:B19.

5. Select the range C13:H19 and press Ctrl+1 to display the Format Cells dialog box. Select the Custom category on the Number tab and enter the following custom format into the Type field to display only the day of the date:

```
d
```

6. Select C13:H19 again and enter the following array formula by pressing Ctrl+Shift+Enter (not just Enter):

```
=B12-(WEEKDAY(B12)-
  1)+{0;1;2;3;4;5;6}+7*{0,1,2,3,4,5}
```

The formula above consists of four parts. The first is the date for the first day of the month (1st May 2015 in this example). The second is to determine the number of days needed to be subtracted from the first day of the month in order to get the date in the first cell of the calendar, which is cell C13 in this case. The third and final are two arrays of numbers. Add 0 for the first row, 1 for the second row, and so forth in the selected range. Add 7*0 for the first column, 7*1 for the second column, and so forth in the selected range.

7. Select C13:H19 again and do conditional formatting for months that are not equal to May by choosing Home | Styles | Conditional Formatting | New Rule to display the New Formatting Rule dialog box. Select the rule type labeled Use a formula to determine which cells to format and type the following formula into the formula box labeled Format values where this formula is true:

```
=MONTH($B$12)<>MONTH(C13)
```

8. Click Format to display the Format Cells dialog box, select gray color in the Color field on the Font tab. Click OK to close the dialog box.

9. Format the calendar the way you prefer.

If you prefer the days to be displayed horizontally (see Figure 2-6), use the following array formula:

```
=B12-(WEEKDAY(B12)-
  1)+{0,1,2,3,4,5,6}+7*{0;1;2;3;4;5}
```

or

```
=TRANSPOSE(B12-(WEEKDAY(B12)-1)+{0;1;2;3;4;5;6}+
  7*{0,1,2,3,4,5})
```

May, 2015						
Sun	Mon	Tue	Wed	Thu	Fri	Sat
26	27	28	29	30	1	2
3	4	5	6	7	8	9
10	11	12	13	14	15	16
17	18	19	20	21	22	23
24	25	26	27	28	29	30
31	1	2	3	4	5	6

Figure 2-6: A calendar created with days displayed horizontally.

A Yearly Live Calendar

To create a yearly calendar, make eleven copies of the monthly calendar that has been created above. To make a copy, select the monthly calendar and hold down Ctrl while you drag it to other location (see Figure 2-7). Only two changes need to be done on each monthly calendar: one is the month header and the other is the cell reference in the conditional formatting, with the following steps:

1. Change the month header to the respective month and display only the month name (without the year) in the header by using the following number format:

   mmmm

2. With any day selected in the calendar, choose Home | Styles | Conditional Formatting | Manage Rules | Edit Rule. In the formula box labeled Format values where this formula is true, replace the existing absolute reference with the absolute reference that refers to the month header of that particular month.

2015

January

Sun	Mon	Tue	Wed	Thu	Fri	Sat
				1	2	3
4	5	6	7	8	9	10
11	12	13	14	15	16	17
18	19	20	21	22	23	24
25	26	27	28	29	30	31

February

Sun	Mon	Tue	Wed	Thu	Fri	Sat
1	2	3	4	5	6	7
8	9	10	11	12	13	14
15	16	17	18	19	20	21
22	23	24	25	26	27	28

March

Sun	Mon	Tue	Wed	Thu	Fri	Sat
1	2	3	4	5	6	7
8	9	10	11	12	13	14
15	16	17	18	19	20	21
22	23	24	25	26	27	28
29	30	31				

April

Sun	Mon	Tue	Wed	Thu	Fri	Sat
			1	2	3	4
5	6	7	8	9	10	11
12	13	14	15	16	17	18
19	20	21	22	23	24	25
26	27	28	29	30		

May

Sun	Mon	Tue	Wed	Thu	Fri	Sat
					1	2
3	4	5	6	7	8	9
10	11	12	13	14	15	16
17	18	19	20	21	22	23
24	25	26	27	28	29	30
31						

June

Sun	Mon	Tue	Wed	Thu	Fri	Sat
	1	2	3	4	5	6
7	8	9	10	11	12	13
14	15	16	17	18	19	20
21	22	23	24	25	26	27
28	29	30				

July

Sun	Mon	Tue	Wed	Thu	Fri	Sat
			1	2	3	4
5	6	7	8	9	10	11
12	13	14	15	16	17	18
19	20	21	22	23	24	25
26	27	28	29	30	31	

August

Sun	Mon	Tue	Wed	Thu	Fri	Sat
						1
2	3	4	5	6	7	8
9	10	11	12	13	14	15
16	17	18	19	20	21	22
23	24	25	26	27	28	29
30	31					

September

Sun	Mon	Tue	Wed	Thu	Fri	Sat
		1	2	3	4	5
6	7	8	9	10	11	12
13	14	15	16	17	18	19
20	21	22	23	24	25	26
27	28	29	30			

October

Sun	Mon	Tue	Wed	Thu	Fri	Sat
				1	2	3
4	5	6	7	8	9	10
11	12	13	14	15	16	17
18	19	20	21	22	23	24
25	26	27	28	29	30	31

November

Sun	Mon	Tue	Wed	Thu	Fri	Sat
1	2	3	4	5	6	7
8	9	10	11	12	13	14
15	16	17	18	19	20	21
22	23	24	25	26	27	28
29	30					

December

Sun	Mon	Tue	Wed	Thu	Fri	Sat
		1	2	3	4	5
6	7	8	9	10	11	12
13	14	15	16	17	18	19
20	21	22	23	24	25	26
27	28	29	30	31		

Figure 2-7: A live yearly calendar created in a range of cells.

If you need to edit an array formula, execute the following steps:

1. Select any cell in the array formula range.

2. Press F2 or click the Formula bar and make changes to the formula.

3. Press Ctrl+Shift+Enter to accept the changes.

To delete an array formula, select any cell in the array formula range, press Ctrl+/ to select all the cells in the range and press Delete.

How to Return the Address of a Cell or a Range of Cells

To return the address of a cell, say cell L8, enter the following formula into a cell:

```
=ADDRESS(ROW(L8),COLUMN(L8))
```

or

```
=CELL("address",L8)
```

Suppose you have a range named myRange. To return its address, enter the following formula into a cell:

```
=ADDRESS(ROW(myRange),COLUMN(myRange))&":"&ADDRESS(R
  OW(myRange)+ROWS(myRange)-
  1,COLUMN(myRange)+COLUMNS(myRange)-1)
```

The ROW function returns the row number of the top-left cell of myRange. The ROWS function returns the number of rows in myRange. Similar goes to the COLUMN and COLUMNS functions.

The returned address is a text string and can be used with INDIRECT function. For example, with cell A1 containing the returned address of myRange, enter the following formula into a cell to sum the numbers in myRange:

```
=SUM(INDIRECT(A1))
```

The example above is only for demonstration how to use a returned address. To sum the numbers in myRange, you can simply use the following formula:

```
=SUM(myRange)
```

Chapter 3: Working with Data in a Worksheet

How to Select and Manipulate Blank Cells

The main reason of selecting blank cells is to do something the same to all the blank cells. Among the things that can be done to the selected blank cells are:

- To enter the same value

- To enter the same formula

- To define a name

- To change the format (number format, alignment, font, border, and fill)

In the following example, I am going to fill the blank cells in Figure 3-1 with 255 different characters by entering a formula only once.

	A	B	C	D	E	F	G	H	I	J	K	L	M	N	O	P	Q	R
1	1		31		61		91		121		151		181		211		241	
2	2		32		62		92		122		152		182		212		242	
3	3		33		63		93		123		153		183		213		243	
4	4		34		64		94		124		154		184		214		244	
5	5		35		65		95		125		155		185		215		245	
6	6		36		66		96		126		156		186		216		246	
7	7		37		67		97		127		157		187		217		247	
8	8		38		68		98		128		158		188		218		248	
9	9		39		69		99		129		159		189		219		249	
10	10		40		70		100		130		160		190		220		250	
11	11		41		71		101		131		161		191		221		251	
12	12		42		72		102		132		162		192		222		252	
13	13		43		73		103		133		163		193		223		253	
14	14		44		74		104		134		164		194		224		254	
15	15		45		75		105		135		165		195		225		255	
16	16		46		76		106		136		166		196		226			
17	17		47		77		107		137		167		197		227			
18	18		48		78		108		138		168		198		228			
19	19		49		79		109		139		169		199		229			
20	20		50		80		110		140		170		200		230			
21	21		51		81		111		141		171		201		231			
22	22		52		82		112		142		172		202		232			
23	23		53		83		113		143		173		203		233			
24	24		54		84		114		144		174		204		234			
25	25		55		85		115		145		175		205		235			
26	26		56		86		116		146		176		206		236			
27	27		57		87		117		147		177		207		237			
28	28		58		88		118		148		178		208		238			
29	29		59		89		119		149		179		209		239			
30	30		60		90		120		150		180		210		240			

Figure 3-1: To fill 255 blank cells with 255 different characters.

To do so, execute the following steps:

1. Select the range A1:P30.

2. Choose Home | Editing | Find & Select | Go To Special to display the Go To Special dialog box.

3. To select only blank cells in the selected range, choose the option Blanks, and click OK.

4. To select the remaining blank cells in the range R1:R15, hold down Ctrl while click cell R1, and then hold down Shift while click cell R15 (see Figure 3-2).

	A	B	C	D	E	F	G	H	I	J	K	L	M	N	O	P	Q	R
1	1		31		61		91		121		151		181		211		241	
2	2		32		62		92		122		152		182		212		242	
3	3		33		63		93		123		153		183		213		243	
4	4		34		64		94		124		154		184		214		244	
5	5		35		65		95		125		155		185		215		245	
6	6		36		66		96		126		156		186		216		246	
7	7		37		67		97		127		157		187		217		247	
8	8		38		68		98		128		158		188		218		248	
9	9		39		69		99		129		159		189		219		249	
10	10		40		70		100		130		160		190		220		250	
11	11		41		71		101		131		161		191		221		251	
12	12		42		72		102		132		162		192		222		252	
13	13		43		73		103		133		163		193		223		253	
14	14		44		74		104		134		164		194		224		254	
15	15		45		75		105		135		165		195		225		255	
16	16		46		76		106		136		166		196		226			
17	17		47		77		107		137		167		197		227			
18	18		48		78		108		138		168		198		228			
19	19		49		79		109		139		169		199		229			
20	20		50		80		110		140		170		200		230			
21	21		51		81		111		141		171		201		231			
22	22		52		82		112		142		172		202		232			
23	23		53		83		113		143		173		203		233			
24	24		54		84		114		144		174		204		234			
25	25		55		85		115		145		175		205		235			
26	26		56		86		116		146		176		206		236			
27	27		57		87		117		147		177		207		237			
28	28		58		88		118		148		178		208		238			
29	29		59		89		119		149		179		209		239			
30	30		60		90		120		150		180		210		240			

Figure 3-2: Defining selected cells a name by using the Name box.

5. Click the Name box and name the selected blank cells CharSet.

    A name created using the Name box is by default a workbook-level name. To create a worksheet-level name, enter the worksheet's name and an exclamation mark before the name (for example, Sheet3!CharSet).

6. In the selected cells, cell R1 is the active cell (see Figure 3-2). Enter the following formula into the formula bar by pressing Ctrl+Enter:

```
=Char(Q1)
```

This formula is then relatively copied to all the selected cells.

7. Choose Home | Font and select Wingdings. Center the cells and format the cells the way you prefer (see Figure 3-3).

	A	B	C	D	E	F	G	H	I	J	K	L	M	N	O	P	Q	R
1	1		31		61	☐	91	☺	121	☒	151	♋	181	✪	211	☿	241	⇧
2	2		32		62	☁	92	♨	122	✻	152	♌	182	☆	212	♋	242	⇩
3	3		33	✎	63	✌	93	✿	123	✹	153	♍	183	◷	213	☒	243	⇔
4	4		34	✂	64	☜	94	♈	124	●	154	♎	184	◷	214	☒	244	⇕
5	5		35	✄	65	☝	95	♉	125	"	155	♏	185	◷	215	◂	245	↶
6	6		36	✌	66	☛	96	♊	126	"	156	♐	186	◷	216	▸	246	↷
7	7		37	✆	67	☟	97	♋	127	☐	157	♑	187	◷	217	▲	247	↩
8	8		38	✉	68	☞	98	♌	128	◎	158	·	188	◷	218	▼	248	↪
9	9		39	✇	69	☚	99	♍	129	①	159	•	189	◷	219	◶	249	□
10	10		40	☎	70	☛	100	♎	130	②	160	·	190	◷	220	➲	250	□
11	11		41	①	71	✐	101	♏	131	③	161	○	191	◷	221	♁	251	✖
12	12		42	✉	72	✎	102	♐	132	④	162	●	192	◷	222	☯	252	✓
13	13		43	✇	73	♻	103	♑	133	⑤	163	●	193	◷	223	←	253	☒
14	14		44	✇	74	☺	104	♒	134	⑥	164	◉	194	◷	224	→	254	☑
15	15		45	✇	75	☺	105	♓	135	⑦	165	◎	195	✧	225	↑	255	▦
16	16		46	✇	76	☹	106	♈	136	⑧	166	○	196	♉	226	↓		
17	17		47	✇	77	☜	107	☞	137	⑨	167	■	197	♋	227	↖		
18	18		48	☐	78	☀	108	●	138	⑩	168	□	198	♐	228	↗		
19	19		49	☞	79	☕	109	○	139	❶	169	◣	199	♉	229	↙		
20	20		50	▤	80	☛	110	■	140	❷	170	✛	200	♐	230	↘		
21	21		51	▥	81	✈	111	□	141	❸	171	★	201	♐	231	←		
22	22		52	▤	82	✿	112	□	142	❹	172	★	202	♋	232	→		
23	23		53	▦	83	◆	113	□	143	❺	173		203	♋	233	↑		
24	24		54	▩	84	✾	114	□	144	❻	174	✳	204	♋	234	↓		
25	25		55	▣	85	✞	115	∙	145	❼	175	✳	205	♌	235	↖		
26	26		56	☟	86	✠	116	◆	146	❽	176	✚	206	♍	236	↗		
27	27		57	☜	87	✝	117	◆	147	❾	177	✚	207	♍	237	↙		
28	28		58	▭	88	✺	118	❖	148	❿	178	✦	208	♌	238	↘		
29	29		59	▭	89	✿	119	∙	149	⓪	179	♯	209	♋	239	⇦		
30	30		60	▣	90	☾	120	☒	150	♋	180	◆	210	♌	240	⇨		

Figure 3-3: A few steps to create 255 different characters.

Since the formerly blank cells, which are now containing 255 characters, have been named CharSet, they can be easily selected by choosing the name in the Name box. With the cells selected, you can to make some changes. For example, you can display the 255 characters in different font.

How to Auto Fill and Sort Roman Numerals

Excel® recognizes common series names such as months and days of the week. When you enter Mon into a cell and drag the fill handle (at the lower-right corner of the cell) across a range of cells, the range is auto filled with successive days of the week. If you enter a Roman numeral I into a cell and try to auto fill by similarly dragging the fill handle, you will not get the series of I, II, III ….

Auto filling a range with Roman numerals, however, can be done by creating a custom list. With the created custom list, Roman numerals can be sorted accordingly too.

To create a custom list for Roman numerals, execute the following steps:

1. Choose File | Options to display the Excel® Options dialog box.

2. Select the Advanced tab, scroll down, and click the Edit Custom Lists button to display the Custom Lists dialog box.

3. In the Custom lists box, NEW LIST is selected by default. Type a list of Roman numerals I, II, III … into the List entries box.

4. Click Add and OK to close the Custom Lists dialog box.

5. Click OK to close the Excel® Options dialog box.

Auto filling a range of cells with Roman numerals can now be done by executing the following steps:

1. Enter the Roman numeral I or i into a cell.

2. Drag the fill handle of the cell across a range of cells to auto fill it with the Roman numerals.

To sort a range or a table using the newly created custom list of Roman numerals, execute the following steps:

1. Select the range of cells to be sorted.

2. Choose Data | Sort & Filter | Sort to display the Sort dialog box.

30

3. From the Order drop-down list, choose Custom List to display the Custom Lists dialog box.

   Without choosing Custom List, the selected range would only be sorted alphabetically, which is not what you want.

4. Select the newly created list of Roman numerals in the Custom lists box.

5. Click OK to close the Custom Lists dialog box and click OK again to close the Sort dialog box.

How to Create a Data Validation List Without Occupying Any Cells

To create a data validation list without occupying any cells, execute the following steps:

1. Select the range that you want to set up the data validation rule.

2. Choose Data | Data Tools | Data Validation to display the Data Validation dialog box.

3. The Settings tab is the default tab. In the Allow field, select List.

4. Type a list of your items, separated by commas, into the Source field. For example, type S,M,L into the Source filed.

5. Place a check mark next to the In-Cell drop-down check box.

6. Optional. If you want an input message to be displayed when a cell in the selected range is activated, select the Input Message tab and specify your message.

7. Optional. If you want to have your own custom error message when an invalid entry is entered, select the Error Alert tab and specify your message.

8. Click OK to close the Data Validation dialog box.

How to Create a Dependent or Cascading Data Validation List

Figure 3-4 shows an example of a dependent or cascading data validation list in cell B3. The drop-down list in cell B3 depends on what is in cell A3. Depending on the values in column A, each cell in column B when activated will appropriately display one of the three drop-down dependent lists, namely the Veggie, Fruit, and Diary lists.

	A	B	C	D	E	F	G
1	**Product**	**Item**					
2	Fruit	Banana				**Dependent lists**	
3	Veggie				**Veggie**	**Fruit**	**Diary**
4	Diary				Asparagus	Apple	Butter
5	Veggie				Broccoli	Apricot	Cheese
6	Fruit				Carrot	Banana	Yogurt
7					Cauliflower	Lemon	
8					Ginger	Orange	
9					Pumpkin	Peach	
10					Sweet Corn		
11							

Figure 3-4: The list in cell B3 depends on the value in cell A3.

To create the result in Figure 3-4, execute the following steps:

1. Prepare the three dependent lists and name the lists respectively Veggie, Fruit, and Diary by following these steps:

   - Enter Veggie into cell E3 and enter a list of veggies into the range E4:E10.

   - Select the range E3:E10 and choose Formulas | Defined Names | Create from Selection to display the Create Names from Selection dialog box.

   - Tick the Top row check box and click OK to name the range E4:E10 Veggie.

- Repeat the steps above to create the other two lists with the respective names of Fruit and Diary (see Figure 3-4).

2. Create data validation lists in column A using the names of the newly created lists by following these steps:

   - In this example, select only the range A2:A11 and choose Data | Data Tools | Data Validation to display the Data Validation dialog box.

   - The Settings tab is the default tab. In the Allow field, select List and type the following list into the Source field:

   ```
   =Veggie, Fruit, Diary
   ```

   - Tick the In-Cell drop-down check box and click OK.

3. Create dependent data validation lists in column B by following these steps:

   - In this example, select only the range B2:B11 and choose Data | Data Tools | Data Validation to display the Data Validation dialog box.

   - The Settings tab is the default tab. In the Allow field, select List and type the following formula into the Source field:

   ```
   =INDIRECT($A2)
   ```

   - Tick the In-Cell drop-down check box and click OK.

How to Highlight Respective Rows When an Item from a List is Selected

This can be accomplished by using conditional formatting. Figure 3-5 shows an example. When an item is selected from the list in cell H2, if it matches the values in column C, the corresponding rows in the range B2:E8 are highlighted.

	B	C	D	E	F	G	H
2	1	Carrot	89	5		Highlighting rows with:	Ginger
3	2	Ginger	79	44			
4	3	Broccoli	7	53			
5	4	Potato	45	60			
6	6	Asparagus	93	71			
7	7	Ginger	40	50			
8	8	Potato	52	87			

Figure 3-5: Any row to be highlighted in the range B2:E8 is based on what is selected in cell H2.

To create the result in Figure 3-5, execute the following steps:

1. Select the range B2:E8, in which rows are to be highlighted, if any.

2. Choose Home | Styles | Conditional Formatting | New Rule to display the New Formatting Rule dialog box.

3. Select the rule type labeled Use a formula to determine which cells to format and type the following formula into the formula box:

```
=$C2=$H$2
```

Note that $C2 is a mixed reference. Hence, its column part is fixed and its row part is allowed to vary during the evaluation of the formula above for every cell in the selected range B2:E8. For example, during the evaluation of the formula above for cell B7, the formula has actually become =$C7=$H$2.

4. Click the Format button and choose the format that you want to apply if the formula returns TRUE.

5. Click OK twice to complete the conditional formatting.

How to Instantly Visualize Values Without Creating an Embedded Chart

Values can be instantly visualized by creating sparklines (normally for data that is arranged horizontally) and data bars (normally for data that is arranged vertically).

To create sparklines for a range of data, execute the following steps:

1. Select the range of cells containing values (for example, C3:N6 as in Figure 3-6).

	B	C	D	E	F	G	H	I	J	K	L	M	N
1						Units Sold							
2	Sales Agent	Jan	Feb	Mar	Apr	May	Jun	Jul	Aug	Sep	Oct	Nov	Dec
3	Bob	6	6	4	10	7	6	10	5	3	6	9	7
4	Jane	6	9	6	5	10	7	9	7	5	10	8	7
5	Kathy	10	8	6	6	10	10	6	6	7	5	7	5
6	Stan	5	9	3	9	9	7	6	9	6	8	7	7
7	Total	27	32	19	30	36	30	31	27	21	29	31	26

Figure 3-6: A range of data for sparklines.

2. Choose Insert | Sparklines | Column to display the Create Sparklines dialog box.

3. In the Data Range field, it shows the range that you have selected (C3:N6 in this case). By default the cursor is in the Location Range field. Select the range of cells that you want the sparklines to be created (for example, O3:O6).

4. Click OK to create the sparklines.

To create data bars for a range of data, execute the following steps:

1. Select the range of cells containing values.

2. Choose Home | Styles | Conditional Formatting | Data Bars | Blue Data Bar.

3. The data bars are created instantly using the default settings. To change the settings, choose Home | Styles | Conditional Formatting | More Rules.

How to Import Data from a Web Page

Importing data from a text file can easily be done by choosing Data | Get External Data | From Text. Here we will explore a less commonly discussed but interesting importing method – importing data from a web page.

To import data from a web page, execute the following steps:

1. Select a cell where you want to put the imported data.

2. Choose Data | Get External Data | From Web to display the New Web Query dialog box.

3. In the Address field, type or paste the URL of the web page.

4. Press Enter or click the Go button.

5. Tables that can be imported are with yellow arrows. To import a table, click the yellow arrow of that table. Once it is clicked, it changes to a green box with a check mark. Repeat the same action for other tables that you want to import.

6. Click the Import button to display the Import Data dialog box.

7. Click OK to import the data to the location that you have selected in Step 1.

Imported data from a web page can be refreshed for any updates. To refresh, right-click any cell in the range of the imported data and choose Refresh.

How to Filter a Table of Data Using Multiple Criteria

Filtering a table is to display only rows of records that meet certain criteria. A criterion can be either text, number, date, or formula based. For example, a criterion can be selecting only records with text containing certain characters, with numbers greater than a particular value, with dates greater than a particular date, or with text, numbers, and/or dates that meet certain rules determined by a formula.

In filtering a table with multiple criteria, all these criteria are pairwise connected either by a logical AND or OR operator. For example, a criterion of selecting only records with text containing certain characters can be connected with a logical AND with another criterion of selecting only records with numbers greater than a particular value (see Figure 3-8).

The examples in this section use a table of fictitious employee data, which has 100 rows of records, for discussions on various criteria (see Figure 3-7).

	B	C	D	E	F	G	H
	Name	Date	Age	Division	Jan Sales	Feb Sales	MC
10							
11	Alec	1 Oct 12	23	AC	8436	9073	3
12	Arthur	3 Aug 11	36	AC	15536	15415	9
13	Elmo	11 Apr 14	20	AC	6732	8252	3
14	Gisela	21 Oct 14	25	AC	6588	8556	25
15	Holmes	17 Jan 16	23	AC	9503	7472	12
16	Hyatt	19 May 14	30	AC	7903	6119	4
17	Ifeoma	27 Feb 15	27	AC	5456	5751	3
18	Jenny	17 Oct 12	26	AC	8303	8400	6
19	John	17 Aug 16	37	AC	15454	19501	7
20	Johnny	18 Jun 12	24	AC	8974	8878	3
21	Jordan	10 Feb 12	39	AC	19484	16010	9
22	Julian	17 Dec 14	27	AC	8886	8522	9
23	Kenyon	2 Sep 12	31	AC	6391	9670	0
24	Kiona	11 Nov 14	21	AC	7788	7503	0

Figure 3-7: Portion of a table of fictitious employee data.

Connecting Criteria with Logical ANDs

If filtering a table involves only logical ANDs in connecting text, number, and date selection criteria, standard filtering does the job efficiently.

To filter a table using standard filtering, execute the following steps:

1. Activate any cell within the table by selecting a cell within the table.

2. Choose Data | Sort & Filter | Filter to display the Filter buttons on the headers of the table.

3. Click one of the Filter buttons for your first criterion. Depending on the data type in the column of the table, select either Text Filters, Date Filters, or Number Filters and set your criterion.

4. Repeat Step 3 for other criteria, if needed.

To clear the filtered result, click the Filter command in the Ribbon.

For example, Figure 3-8 shows a filtered result with names started with J and ended with y and with ages greater than 25.

	B	C	D	E	F	G	H
10	Name	Date	Age	Division	Jan Sales	Feb Sales	MC
18	Jenny	17 Oct 12	26	AC	8303	8400	6
39	Jeremy	4 Jun 13	30	DR	8949	6379	4
111							

Figure 3-8: Records with names started with J and ended with y and with ages greater than 25.

Connecting Criteria with Logical ORs

If filtering a table involves logical ORs in connecting selection criteria, advanced filtering is needed. Rows above the table are known as criteria range and they are used to set the criteria (see Figure 3.9). The first row in the criteria range is for field names (known as criteria labels), which are the headers of the table. Leave at least one blank row between the criteria range and the table.

A row in a criteria range can have any number of criteria, each of which is connected with others by a logical AND. And in a criteria range, it can have any number of rows, each of which is connected with others by a logical OR (see Figure 3-9 and Figure 3-10).

The ways to enter number and formula selection criteria are more intuitive than text and date selection criteria. Hence, Table 3-1 shows some examples of ways to enter text and date selection criteria.

Table 3-1: Examples of text and date selection criteria

Criterion	What to enter into a cell
Text equals John	'=John or ="=John"
Text does not equal John	'<>John or <>John
Text begins with Jo	'=Jo*, Jo, or Jo*
Text ends with ny	'=*ny
Text contains ny	'=*ny*, '*ny*, '*ny, *ny*, or *ny
Text does not contain ny	'<>*ny* or <>*ny*
Text does not begin with Jo	'<>Jo* or <>Jo*
Text does not end with ny	'<>*ny or <>*ny
Text starts with J and ends with y	'=J*y
Text contains n, any character, and y	'=*n?y*
Text contains only 3 characters	'=???
Text does not contain 3 characters	'<>??? or <>???
A date equals Oct 21, 2014	="="&DATE(2014,10,21)
A date after Oct 21, 2014	=">"&DATE(2014,10,21)
A date after or equals Oct 21, 2014	=">="&DATE(2014,10,21)

Figure 3-9 shows an example of how to find records that meet multiple criteria in one column of the table, namely the Name column. It shows only those records with names started with J and ended with y, or with names started with Ki.

To get the filtered result, execute the following steps:

1. Enter the text selection criteria into the criteria range as shown in Figure 3-9.

   A text selection criterion is not case sensitive. Ki is the same as KI. For case-sensitive text search, a formula (the EXACT function) is needed.

2. Activate any cell within the table.

3. Choose Data | Sort & Filter | Advanced to display the Advanced Filter dialog box.

4. In the List range field, it automatically shows the range of the table. Click the Criteria range field and select the range B1:B3.

5. Click OK to apply the filter to the table (Figure 3-9).

To clear the filtered result, click the Clear command in the Ribbon.

	B	C	D	E	F	G	H
1	Name						
2	=J*y						
3	ki						
9							
10	Name	Date	Age	Division	Jan Sales	Feb Sales	MC
18	Jenny	17 Oct 12	26	AC	8303	8400	6
20	Johnny	18 Jun 12	24	AC	8974	8878	3
24	Kiona	11 Nov 14	21	AC	7788	7503	0
25	Kirestin	7 Dec 13	34	AC	16449	16625	5
39	Jeremy	4 Jun 13	30	DR	8949	6379	4
111							

Figure 3-9: Names started with J and ended with y, or started with Ki.

You might aware that standard filtering can also find records that meet multiple criteria in one column in certain circumstances, but only with one logical OR. For example it can filter records with names started with Ki or containing nn, but it cannot get the filtered result in Figure 3-9. Hence, advanced filtering offers greater flexibility.

Connecting Criteria with Logical ANDs and ORs

Suppose you want to find out which rows of records that meet one of the following two conditions:

- Employees that have joined the company since 2011 with MC not greater than 5 and with Feb Sales of at least 15000

    or

- Employees with Feb Sales greater than 18000

To get the result, execute the following steps:

1. Enter the selection criteria into the criteria range as shown in Figure 3-10.

    The date selection criterion is with the following formula:

    `="<="&DATE(2011,12,31)`

2. Activate any cell within the table.

3. Choose Data | Sort & Filter | Advanced to display the Advanced Filter dialog box.

4. In the List range field, it shows the range of the table. Click the Criteria range field and select the range B1:D3.

5. Click OK to apply the filter to the table (Figure 3-10).

To clear the filtered result, click the Clear command in the Ribbon.

	B	C	D	E	F	G	H
1	**Date**	**MC**	**Feb Sales**				
2	<=40908	<=5	>=15000				
3			>=18000				
9							
10	**Name**	**Date**	**Age**	**Division**	**Jan Sales**	**Feb Sales**	**MC**
19	John	17 Aug 16	37	AC	15454	19501	7
26	Lacey	27 Aug 11	35	AC	16843	17424	3
50	Chastity	6 May 15	36	HM	16000	18553	13
102	Joel	17 Oct 11	37	QR	19578	19202	10
111							

Figure 3-10: Connecting criteria with two logical ANDs and one logical OR.

Creating Criteria Using Formulas

Criteria labels for criteria using formulas can be either blank or descriptive, as long as the descriptive labels are not the same as the field names of the table to be filtered. A criterion formula must use a relative reference that refers to the cell (or cells) in the first data row of the table.

Suppose you want to find out which rows of records in AC Division with at least 10% increase in Feb Sales as compared to Jan Sales. To get the result, execute the following steps:

1. Enter the selection criteria into the criteria range as shown in Figure 3-11.

   The formula selection criterion is with the following formula:

   `=G11>=F11*1.1`

2. Activate any cell within the table.

3. Choose Data | Sort & Filter | Advanced to display the Advanced Filter dialog box.

4. In the List range field, it shows the range of the table. Click the Criteria range field and select the range B1:C2.

5. Click OK to apply the filter to the table (Figure 3-11).

To clear the filtered result, click the Clear command in the Ribbon.

	B	C	D	E	F	G	H
1	**Division**	**10% up**					
2	=AC	FALSE					
9							
10	**Name**	**Date**	**Age**	**Division**	**Jan Sales**	**Feb Sales**	**MC**
13	Elmo	11 Apr 14	20	AC	6732	8252	3
14	Gisela	21 Oct 14	25	AC	6588	8556	25
19	John	17 Aug 16	37	AC	15454	19501	7
23	Kenyon	2 Sep 12	31	AC	6391	9670	0
28	Leandra	12 Jan 14	24	AC	6161	7681	12
30	Ryan	15 May 14	37	AC	12004	14268	3

Figure 3-11: Rows of records involving a formula selection criterion.

Chapter 4: Worksheets and Files

How to Use Form and ActiveX Controls on a Worksheet

Excel® provides two types of controls that can be placed on a worksheet. Form controls are built-in to Excel® and easier to use. ActiveX controls on the other hand are loaded separately and offer greater flexibility in which you can access extensive properties to customize their appearances and behavior. However, computers by default do not trust ActiveX controls and issue a security warning.

The bottom line is to use only Form controls if ActiveX controls are not needed to accomplish the task.

To have functional controls on a worksheet, execute the following steps:

1. Choose Developer | Controls | Insert to select a control. Draw the control by dragging the mouse pointer at the location where you want it to be placed on the worksheet.

    If the Developer tab is not available, choose File | Options to display the Excel® Options dialog box. Select the Customize Ribbon tab, tick the Developer check box, and click OK.

2. To set the properties of a Form control, right-click the control and choose Format Control to display the Control tab of the Format Control dialog box.

    To set the properties of an ActiveX control, right-click the control and choose Properties to display the Properties window.

    Note that before the properties of an ActiveX control can be set, Excel® must be in design mode. Choose Developer | Controls | Design Mode to set Excel® in design mode.

    Table 4-1 shows the common properties that need to be set after a control is placed on a worksheet.

Table 4-1: The common properties of Form and ActiveX controls

Form control	ActiveX control
Combox box • Input range • Cell link	Combox box • ListFillRange • LinkedCell
List box • Input range • Cell link	List box • ListFillRange • LinkedCell
Spinner • Min • Max • Incremental change • Cell link	Spinner • Min • Max • SmallChange • LinkedCell
Scroll bar • Min • Max • Incremental change • Page change • Cell link	Scroll bar • Min • Max • SmallChange • LargeChange • LinkedCell
Radio button • Cell link	Radio button • LinkedCell
Check box • Cell link	Check box • LinkedCell

3. Move and resize the control necessarily. Table 4-2 shows the way how to select and resize a control.

Table 4-2: How to select and resize a control

Action	Form control	ActiveX control
Selecting a control	Click the control while hold down Ctrl; or right-click the control and press Esc.	Click the control when Excel® is in design mode.
Fitting a control to the height and width of a range	Resize the control while hold down Alt. To resize the control without holding down Alt, choose Format | Arrange | Align | Snap to Grid.	

The best way to get familiarized with the usage of controls on a worksheet is working through an example. Figure 4-1 shows an example of an interactive worksheet, which incorporates a combo box and two scroll bars to find the monthly repayment amount on a car loan. The user can select the car model in the combo box and change the interest rate and repayment period by using the two scroll bars.

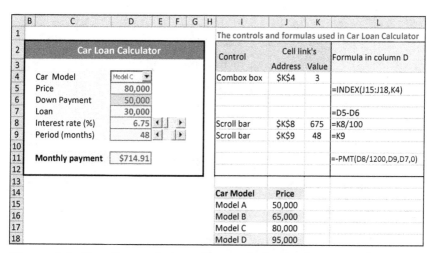

Figure 4-1: Creating an interactive worksheet using controls.

To create the interactive car loan calculator in Figure 4-1, execute the following steps:

1. Place one combo box and two scroll bars on the worksheet (see Figure 4-1).

2. Set their properties as shown in Table 4-3.

Table 4-3: The properties (and their values) of the controls used in Figure 4-1

Control	Property and value
Combo box	Input range: $I$15:$I$18 Cell link: $K$4
Scroll bar for the interest rate	Min: 0 Max: 1000 Incremental change: 25 Page change: 100 Cell link: $K$8
Scroll bar for the repayment period	Min: 1 Max: 48 Incremental change: 1 Page change: 10 Cell link: $K$9

3. Enter the following formula into cell D5:

```
=INDEX(J15:J18,K4)
```

The car price will then be automatically displayed in cell D5.

4. In cell D7, the loan amount is calculated with the following formula:

```
=D5-D6
```

5. In cell D8, the interest rate in percent is calculated from the value of the scroll bar with the following formula:

    ```
    =K8/100
    ```

    Cell K8 is the linked cell to the scroll bar for the interest rate.

6. Enter the following formula into cell D9:

    ```
    =K9
    ```

    Cell K9 is the linked cell to the scroll bar for the repayment period.

7. Enter following formula into cell D11 to calculate the monthly payment on the car loan:

    ```
    =-PMT(D8/1200,D9,D7,0)
    ```

8. Hide columns I to L.

Sometimes you want a control undeleted even if its underlying cell is deleted. To do so, right-click the control and choose Format Control to display the Format Control dialog box. Select the Properties tab and make sure the option Move and size with cells is either grayed out or unselected.

The underlying cell of a control is identified by the location of the upper leftmost corner of the control. To facilitate the identification, hold down Alt as you move the control.

How to Hide Sheets so an Average User Is Not Able to Unhide It

1. Press Alt+F11 to display the Visual Basic® Editor.

2. Select the sheet that you want to hide in the Project Explorer window.

3. Press F4 to display the Properties window.

4. Look for the property named Visible and choose xlSheetVeryHidden.

How to Reduce the Size of an Excel® File

Four possible ways of reducing the file size are discussed in this section:

Resetting the Last Cell

You can locate the last cell of an active worksheet by pressing Ctrl+End. If the last cell is not what you think it's supposed to be, joint down this last cell (say cell ABC88888). It will be used to reset to the last cell to the actual last cell (say cell AB123).

To reset the last cell (from cell ABC88888 to cell AB123), delete the excess rows and columns by executing the following steps:

1. Create a backup of your file just in case you need it back after the deletion of rows and columns.

2. Enter AC:ABC into the Name box to select the columns AC:ABC.

3. Choose Home | Cells | Delete to delete the excess columns.

4. Repeat Steps 2 and 3 to delete the excess rows of 124:88888.

5. Save, close, and reopen the file.

Deleting Unwanted Hidden Sheets

To unhide any hidden sheets, right-click any sheet tab, and choose Unhide to display the Unhide dialog box. Unhide and delete any wanted hidden sheets.

However, some hidden sheets are much hidden and cannot be unhidden in such a way. To unhide such hidden sheets, execute the following steps:

1. Press Alt+F11 to display the Visual Basic® Editor.

2. In the Project Explorer window, select the sheet that cannot be unhidden in the way described above.

3. Press F4 to activate the Properties window.

4. Look for the property named Visible and change xlSheetVeryHidden to xlSheetVisible.

5. Repeat Steps 2 to 4 for other hidden sheets, if any.

6. Switch back to Excel® by pressing Alt+Tab.

7. Delete the unwanted sheets.

Deleting Unwanted Hidden Objects

Pictures, shapes, text boxes, diagrams, charts, Form controls, and ActiveX controls are examples of objects that are possibly hidden in a worksheet. To find out if you have hidden objects in a worksheet, choose Home | Editing | Find & Select | Selection Pane to display the Selection pane.

Select any hidden object in the list, make it visible, and press Delete if it is unwanted. To delete all objects in the list, press F5 or Ctrl+G, choose Special, select Objects option, click OK, and press Delete.

Tracking Down the Culprits

If the three ways above did not reduce the file size considerably, try to rename the Excel® file by adding a zip extension. Use Windows® Explorer to explore the folders and files in the zip file. First, check the size of each worksheet in the folder named worksheets and the size of each chart sheet, if any, in the folder named chartsheets. If nothing suspicious is found, only then check other files in other folders. Delete unnecessary components, if you know what they are. Once complete, delete the zip extension to reset the file back to an Excel® file.

Chapter 5: VBA

How to Make Your VBA Code to Run Faster

Working with Arrays Instead of a Range of Cells

VBA and Excel® are two different entities. VBA code that repeatedly switches between the two will greatly increase the execution time. A better approach is to copy the entire range once into an array, to work with that array, and to write back the result to the worksheet. This will greatly reduce the number of times that the VBA code needs to switch between these two entities.

Let's compare the execution times between these two approaches. Suppose you want to count the number of numbers that are divisible by four in a range of 50,000 cells. The code that works with an array is generally faster than the one switches between VBA and Excel®. Table 5-1 shows the results of my tests. Code 5-1 and Code 5-2 are the examples of VBA code.

Table 5-1: Execution times (in seconds) for two different approaches in counting the number of numbers that are divisible by four in a range of 50,000 cells

Working with a range of cells	Working with an array
0.20	0.031

Code 5-1: An example of VBA code that works with a range of cells.

```
Sub WorkingWithRange()
'To Count the number of numbers that are divisible by 4
'in a range of 50,000 cells.
Dim r As Long,
Dim c As Long
Dim rN As Long
Dim cN As Long
Dim cnt As Long
Dim StartTimer As Date
Dim EndTimer As Date
    StartTimer = Timer
```

```
      rN = 500:    cN = 100:    cnt = 0
      For r = 1 To rN
          For c = 1 To cN
              If Sheets(1).Cells(r, c) Mod 4 = 0 Then _
                  cnt = cnt + 1
          Next c
      Next r
      EndTimer = Timer
      Debug.Print cnt
      Debug.Print EndTimer - StartTimer
End Sub
```

Code 5-2: An example of much faster VBA code that works with an array.

```
Sub WorkingWithAnArray()
'To count the number of numbers that are divisible by 4
'in a range of 50,000 cells.
Dim x() As Variant
Dim r As Long
Dim c As Long
Dim rN As Long
Dim cN As Long
Dim cnt As Long
Dim StartTimer As Date
Dim EndTimer As Date
      StartTimer = Timer
      rN = 500:    cN = 100:    cnt = 0
      ReDim x(rN, cN)
      Sheets(1).Activate
      x = Range("A1").Resize(rN, cN)
      For r = 1 To rN
          For c = 1 To cN
              If x(r, c) Mod 4 = 0 Then cnt = cnt + 1
          Next c
      Next r
      EndTimer = Timer
      Debug.Print cnt
      Debug.Print EndTimer - StartTimer
End Sub
```

55

VBA code that works within the same worksheet is generally faster than the one that works with multiple worksheets. The execution time can be shorten further if arrays are used. Table 5-2 shows the results of my tests. Code 5-3, Code 5-4, and Code 5-5 are the examples of VBA code.

Table 5-2: Execution times (in seconds) for three different approaches in finding and displaying the numbers that are divisible by four in a range of 50,000 cells

Working with multiple worksheets	Working within the same worksheet	Working within the same worksheet using arrays
0.47	0.45	0.047

Code 5-3: An example of VBA code that works with multiple worksheets.

```
Sub WorkingWithMultipleSheets()
'To find and display the numbers that are divisible by 4
'in a range of 50,000 cells.
Dim r As Long
Dim c As Long
Dim rN As Long
Dim cN As Long
Dim cnt As Long
Dim StartTimer As Date
Dim EndTimer As Date
    StartTimer = Timer
    rN = 500:    cN = 100:    cnt = 0
    For r = 1 To rN
        For c = 1 To cN
            With Sheets(1)
                If .Cells(r, c) Mod 4 = 0 Then
                    cnt = cnt + 1
                    'Paste the number in the 2nd sheet
                    Sheets(2).Cells(cnt,1)=.Cells(r,c)
                End If
            End With
```

```
            Next c
        Next r
        EndTimer = Timer
        Debug.Print cnt
        Debug.Print EndTimer - StartTimer
End Sub
```

Code 5-4: An example of faster VBA code that works within the same worksheet.

```
Sub WorkingWithinSameSheetUsingRange()
'To find and display the numbers that are divisible by 4
'in a range of 50,000 cells.
Dim r As Long
Dim c As Long
Dim rN As Long
Dim cN As Long
Dim cnt As Long
Dim StartTimer As Date
Dim EndTimer As Date
        StartTimer = Timer
        rN = 500:   cN = 100:   cnt = 0
        For r = 1 To rN
            For c = 1 To cN
                With Sheets(1)
                    If .Cells(r, c) Mod 4 = 0 Then
                        cnt = cnt + 1
                        'Paste the number in column A in the
                        'same sheet
                        .Cells(cnt + rN, 1) = .Cells(r, c)
                    End If
                End With
            Next c
        Next r
        EndTimer = Timer
        Debug.Print cnt
        Debug.Print EndTimer - StartTimer
End Sub
```

Code 5-5: An example of much faster VBA code that works within the same worksheet using arrays.

```
Sub WorkingWithinSameSheetUsingArrays()
'To find and display the numbers that are divisible by 4
'in a range of 50,000 cells.
'Notes: The arrays below are one-based arrays.
'The statement Option Base 1 is in the Declaration,
'the part before the 1st procedure.
Dim x() As Variant
Dim out() As Long   'or Variant
Dim r As Long
Dim c As Long
Dim rN As Long
Dim cN As Long
Dim cnt As Long
Dim StartTimer As Date
Dim EndTimer As Date
    StartTimer = Timer
    rN = 500:   cN = 100:   cnt = 0
    ReDim x(rN, cN)
    ReDim out(1 To rN * cN, 1 To 1)
    Sheets(1).Activate
    x = Range("A1").Resize(rN, cN)
    For r = 1 To rN
        For c = 1 To cN
            If x(r, c) Mod 4 = 0 Then
                cnt = cnt + 1
                out(cnt, 1) = x(r, c)
            End If
        Next c
    Next r
    'Paste the numbers in column B in the same sheet
    Sheets(1).Range("B" & rN + 1).Resize(cnt, 1) = out
    EndTimer = Timer
    Debug.Print cnt
    Debug.Print EndTimer - StartTimer
End Sub
```

Disabling Screen Updating, Alert Displays, Events, and Automatic Calculations

If they are not necessary during the execution of your VBA code, disable them before the execution and restore them to their initial settings right before the execution ends. Restoring the settings rather than turning them all on is a good practice since some users may have different settings (see Code 5-6).

Code 5-6: Disabling screen updating, alert displays, events, and automatic calculations.

```
'Declaration
Dim ScrnU As Boolean, DispA As Boolean
Dim Evnt As Boolean, Calc As Long

'Save the settings
With Application
    ScrnU = .ScreenUpdating
    DispA = .DisplayAlerts
    Evnt = .EnableEvents
    Calc = .Calculation
End With

'Disable them before the execution begins
With Application
    .ScreenUpdating = False
    .DisplayAlerts = False
    .EnableEvents = False
    .Calculation = xlCalculationManual
End With

'Here runs your code

'Restore the initial settings before the execution ends
With Application
    .ScreenUpdating = ScrnU
    .DisplayAlerts = DispA
    .EnableEvents = Evnt
    .Calculation = Calc
End With
```

Chapter 6: Some Useful Keys and Shortcuts

Cell or range related action	Key or shortcut
To copy.	Ctrl+C
To paste.	Ctrl+V
To paste special.	Alt+E, S
To undo.	Ctrl+Z
To select entire column or columns.	Ctrl+Spacebar
To select entire row or rows.	Shift+Spacebar
To select the current region of a cell.	Ctrl+A
To select all the cells in a worksheet, if the active cell is not in a current region/table.	Ctrl+A
To select a table without its headers, if the active cell is within the table.	Ctrl+A
To select the whole table (with headers).	Ctrl+A twice
To select the range of an array formula.	Ctrl+/
To select a range of cells.	Hold down Shift while click the other end of the range.
To do multiple selections.	Hold down Ctrl while select other ranges.
To move around in a selected range of cells.	Tab or Shift+Tab or Enter or Shift+Enter
To jump around in a worksheet. You may reach the boundary of the worksheet in one or a few keystrokes.	Ctrl+Arrow
To jump to the last cell.	Ctrl+End

To select the range from the current active cell to the last cell.	Ctrl+Shift+End
To enter a line break in a cell.	Alt+Enter
To jump to the next word in a cell.	Ctrl+Right Arrow
To jump to the previous word in a cell.	Ctrl+Left Arrow
To apply or remove bold formatting.	Ctrl+B
To apply or remove underlining formatting.	Ctrl+U
To apply or remove italic formatting.	Ctrl+I

Formula related action	Key or shortcut
To edit a cell content.	Double-click or F2
To enter a line break in a formula. This does not affect the evaluation of the formula.	Alt+Enter
To enter the same value or formula in the selected range of cells.	Ctrl+Enter
To enter an array formula.	Ctrl+Shift+Enter
To evaluate a selected part of a formula (for example, 1+2, in 1+2+4 returns 3+4).	F9
To select an item from an AutoComplete list.	Down or Up Arrow and Tab
To insert current date.	Ctrl+;
To enter a fraction.	0 and a space
To switch between relative, absolute, and mixed references.	F4
To toggle the height of the Formula bar.	Ctrl+Shift+U

To toggle between Formula view and Normal view.	Ctrl+`

Dialog box related action	Key or shortcut
To display the Format Cells dialog box.	Ctrl+1
To display the Go To dialog box.	F5 or Ctrl+G
To display the Name Manager.	Ctrl+F3

Sheet related action	Key or shortcut
To activate previous sheet.	Ctrl+PgUp
To activate next sheet.	Ctrl+PgDn

Ribbon related action	Key or shortcut
To access a control in the Ribbon.	Alt and pop-up keystrokes
To repeatedly apply Format Painter. Click again Format Painter to disable this sticky feature.	Double-click Format Painter
To save the file.	Ctrl+S

Chart related action	Key or shortcut
To instantly create an embedded chart.	Alt+F1

VBA related action	Key or shortcut
To display the Visual Basic® Editor.	Alt+F11
To display the Immediate window.	Ctrl+G
To display the Properties window.	F4
To halt the execution of a VBA code.	Ctrl+Break

To learn some other common shortcut keys, try to search for the words keyboard shortcuts in Microsoft® Excel® Help window. Press F1 for help.

www.ingramcontent.com/pod-product-compliance
Lightning Source LLC
Chambersburg PA
CBHW061051050326
40690CB00012B/2574